ONE TRUTH, ONE LAW:
I AM, I CREATE

Erin Werley

ISBN 978-1-7343638-0-7 (Paperback Edition)

ISBN 978-0-578-49909-3 (Ebook Edition)

One Truth, One Law: I Am, I Create / Erin Werley

Editing by Melanie Votaw
Cover image by rendix_alextian
Cover design by Jason Anscomb

January 2020.
Published by MadLeo Publishing LLC.
P.O. Box 4053
Hammond, IN 46324

Dedication

This book is for you.
You are more powerful than
you've ever imagined.

CONTENTS

INTRODUCTION BY ERIN

I know you feel lost sometimes. I know you wonder who you really are and why you're here. I know sometimes it feels like everybody else has it figured out, while you're sitting on the sidelines.

I know this because I used to feel the same way. I was in my late twenties, but I was still that same scared girl who had been picked on in school and always felt alone, no matter how many people were around me. I always felt like everyone else had it figured out, and the best I could do was pretend to be like them.

I didn't trust myself, so I trusted other people to give me advice about what I should do with my life. I'd never stood up to anyone, ever. At least not about anything important. Basically, I was a mess.

But I felt something. I knew there had to be more to life. So I read self-improvement books—lots of books. I started thinking more positive thoughts. I started to love myself a little more, bit by bit.

Then, one day, I saw a channeler on the internet and read one of her books. She seemed to understand life in a way I didn't—all because she had a secret weapon. Somebody who knew what was really going on was contacting her from another dimension! I wished I could do that, but I didn't believe it was possible. I mean, who was I, anyway? Why would an advanced being waste time on me?

So I kept reading books, trying to figure out the meaning of life and figure out if there was a purpose to it all.

One night, everything I'd been reading just clicked, and I wrote in a notebook *We are all God* and *We are all one.* Full disclosure: I had no idea what that meant when I wrote it down, but it came out of me onto the paper. I went to sleep, thinking nothing of it.

The next day, in the shower, I remembered what I had written the previous night, and I asked, out loud, "Am I God?" I wasn't expecting an answer, but I must have been open to it because I heard a voice in my head say *Yes.* I knew immediately it wasn't my voice. It sounded the same, but I hadn't thought the thought. It was just "deposited" in my mind.

And those "deposits" kept coming.

This book is a series of conversations between my husband Phil and my inner voice. During the summer of 2011, I lay down on the couch in our cramped, one-bedroom apartment in Virginia Beach almost every day. Phil would ask me questions, and my inner voice, who calls itself "I Am," would answer out loud through me. We recorded those conversations on a tape recorder (can you believe we were still using tapes in 2011?) and transcribed them.

We were excited about what we were hearing, but we were young and lacked confidence. I was sure everyone would think I was crazy, so I didn't want to share what I'd learned.

In the eight years since then, I've grown a great deal. So when I pulled the transcripts out of the basement last summer, I was blown away to realize, in retrospect, how much my life had been influenced by what my inner voice had said.

However, this book is not really about me or my husband. It's about you, because your inner voice has been waiting to talk with you throughout your whole life. You remember that feeling of being lost that I mentioned at the beginning? You feel that way because you've been separated from your inner self, who desperately wants to be found.

This book will show you how to tap into that voice. Once you're talking to that wise part of you, you won't need this book anymore. Because you are God, and you don't need anyone else to tell you who you are.

•

INTRODUCTION BY I AM

My name is I Am, but you've probably spent your whole life referring to me as God. My name doesn't matter. What matters is who I am and who you are.

I am everything. I am all that exists.

The nonphysical world is a collection of thoughts. The physical world that you live in is simply a projection of each of those thoughts. Everything that you see, feel, hear, taste, and smell in the physical world has been created by my thoughts.

You are a projection of an almost infinite number of thoughts. Each time you have a new thought, it begins in the nonphysical world and is projected into the physical. What you call your consciousness exists in the nonphysical and is projected into what seems like a real, physical world to you. I am constantly projecting all the thoughts of billions of people into the physical world. I am each of you. Your thoughts are mine. There is no separation. You are God.

You think you are someone else because I, and therefore you, have unlimited creative power. You have the ability to create a persona and believe it's real, that you are an individual. It's not the truth, but since you created it, it exists in the physical world.

There's so much more to know, and I'm so excited to share it with you. But for now, that's enough to get you started. Let's talk about you and why you're holding this book in your hands. You've spent your whole life being lost. Somewhere, no matter how deep down inside, you've always wondered why you're here. Where did you really come from? Why does everyone else seem to have it together while you're just barely holding on? How come they seem to belong to some secret club that already knows all the answers?

There's a reason you're holding this book. Your life experiences and desires led you here. If you have the courage to set aside what you think you know, this book has the answers you've never quite been able to grasp. If you have the courage to read with a truly open mind, you won't ever have to search for the truth again. You will know who you are and why you're here.

In fact, if you follow the prompts in this book, you may begin talking with me yourself. You may begin hearing my answers to your questions in your head. With practice, it is possible. Erin will keep writing more books because it is joyful for her to create them, and it is her purpose. But you should stop reading them once you've begun to hear my answers in your head. At that point, you will be able to find out your purpose and begin to create it. You won't need to know the answers to Erin's and Phil's questions. You'll be able to get the answers to your own questions.

Anyone who tells you they channel something without encouraging you to do so yourself will never lead you to your real answers. They haven't found the truth themselves. This book is all about learning to listen to yourself, your true self, who is God.

I love Erin just as I love all of you. I am always trying to come through to you. Every creative thought you have is me. Every negative, doubting thought you have is your persona. For years, I tried to make contact with Erin through her writing. She would sit down and write in a sort of trance state and have no idea what she was writing. When she was done, she would read something like this and be amazed and wonder where it came from and what it meant.

Dress, why are you dancing?
Because the air moves me.

That's funny, I didn't know dresses could move by themselves.
We don't. We only move when the air moves us, just like you.

What do you mean?
You only move when you're moved.

You mean I don't move me, something else does?
Yes, you're not who you think you are.

Who am I?
You're lost.

That's something Erin wrote long before she found me. I was always trying to get her to listen to me, but her persona was blocking me. Have you ever had an experience like this?

Something you couldn't explain? I would bet you have, because you are me just as much as Erin is, and so I know you've always felt lost in a way you couldn't quite grasp.

I'm always trying to come through to you any way I can. I want to be found. I don't want you to be lost. I want you to know who you are. You are God, and there is nothing more powerful than you. You create your world with your thoughts, whether or not you realize you're doing it. The power that builds universes courses through your veins. You are a living, breathing embodiment of God, and I love you so much.

Please read this book as many times as it takes to begin to understand my words. Then, instead of forgetting about it, practice listening to me yourself. Follow the steps in this book. I've been knocking at the door of your consciousness your whole life, and I'm so excited that you're close to letting me in.

•

DAY 1: THE VOICE

"At the center of your being you have the answer; you know who you are and you know what you want."

Lao Tzu

"You're not going to believe this," I said, standing naked in front of Phil as water dripped off me onto the carpet. "I'm talking to God in my head!"

"What?" Phil asked, glancing away from his video game. As soon as he saw me, he dropped the controller. "What do you mean?"

I walked to the bathroom and grabbed a towel. "I'm not sure. I'm asking questions, and I hear the answer in my head."

"What makes you think it's God?"

"The voice told me it's God. It said I was God."

"What does that mean?"

"I have no idea."

"Can I ask it something?" Phil asked.

Fear slammed through me. Phil has a very open mind, so he'll give any idea a chance. At the same time, he's super analytical. I hadn't heard the voice since I had gotten out of the shower a few minutes earlier. I was already doubting what had happened. If this wasn't God in my head, he'd know right away. My heart started racing and sweat beaded on my upper lip. I wanted to say no. I wanted to run back into the shower and keep it all to myself. I would never be able to answer his questions. Before I could run and hide, I heard the voice again. *Relax. You don't have to answer anything. I love you. Trust me.*

I still wasn't sure. I didn't want to lie to Phil, or pretend to be something I'm not. The voice heard my doubts and said, *Lie down. Close your eyes. Let me do the talking. You don't have to do anything.* I knew that wasn't my voice answering me. I had never known anything with so much certainty.

I lay down on the couch and Phil asked a question. I heard the answer and spoke it out loud. After that, the voice took over, and I didn't hear the answers between the question being asked and the words coming out of my mouth. It felt wonderful to relax and let the voice take over. I felt enveloped in warmth and love. And the voice was right. I didn't have to answer anything. I just had to allow it to flow.

Phil and my inner voice talked for about an hour. At the end, he was convinced the answers were coming from somewhere beyond me, beyond Erin. I was convinced as well, because I could feel the difference the whole time.

We weren't expecting that first conversation, so we didn't record it. This conversation you're about to read is actually our second, which took place the following day. If it feels awkward at times, like Phil's reading from a list of questions, it's because he was. Those first few days, we were both nervous. We didn't want to do anything to mess this up and make I Am go away. Phil wrote questions he thought of during the day so he wouldn't be left with his mouth hanging open, wondering what to say next. When we started to understand how much I Am loves us all, Phil relaxed and the conversations flowed naturally.

•

DAY 2: NO LIMITS

*"If the doors of perception were cleansed
Everything would appear to man as it is, infinite."*

William Blake

PHIL: Who are you?

I AM: I Am. You would probably call me God, but I Am. There's nothing else but me. In the beginning, my mind in the spiritual world was all that existed. The physical world did not exist. Only my thoughts existed, and all of my thoughts created immediately. Then, I thought a physical world, and it was projected from my mind into existence.

PHIL: Is Erin channeling you?

I AM: No. I am Erin's inner voice. Erin is me just like you are me. Every human is me. Every human can access me. When somebody says they're channeling something outside of themselves it's because they don't understand that they are God and that we are all one.

PHIL: If I'm God, why do I worry so much?

I AM: Worry comes from not knowing that you are God and that every thought you have creates.

PHIL: Every thought I have creates?

I AM: Yes. I am everything. We are all one. Through thought, I have created everything in the physical world. It is possible for you to think and create because your inner self is God, whether you know it or not.

That is the one truth, one law: I Am and I create. Each thought I, and therefore, you have creates precisely, every time. There is nothing in the physical world that was not first created in mind. It is true that who you are, what you are surrounded by, and the life you lead is a manifestation of human thoughts, both yours and others. You are what you know, who you believe, and that starts in mind.

I am your inner voice. I am always guiding you, but it is your choice to listen or not. I want you to create a joyful life through knowing intent. I do not want you to feel helpless, as if things happen to you instead of by you.

PHIL: I have a hard time wrapping my head around that.

I AM: You have to accept that when you're hearing this, you might not understand everything right away because the concepts are new to you. Accept that you need to keep reacquainting yourself with them until they are part of you.

That is the process of seeking. There's nothing wrong with it not being completely clear yet. Your understanding will grow as your knowing grows.

PHIL: Okay. Then what is the difference between the truth you mentioned and our thoughts?

I AM: There is only one truth, one law: I Am and I create. This truth exists in the spiritual world of universal mind and cannot be changed through thought. Anything that has been created in the physical world is human-made. It is not the one truth because it can be changed through thought. It only exists until a new creation changes it. A single creative thought can tear that human-made creation down.

PHIL: So human-made creations are limitations?

I AM: Yes. But these limitations allow you to experience your creations in the physical world.

PHIL: Okay. Are laws limitations too?

I AM: Absolutely. There are no limits. People believe there are limits because they do not have knowing that every thought creates. If you aren't creating through a calm knowing that your thoughts create, you are creating through fear.

PHIL: Are all scientific laws limitations?

I AM: That's right. That's why science is always changing and discovering new things. What had previously existed ceases to exist when new thoughts are created.

PHIL: When you refer to a calm knowing, what do you mean?

I AM: Knowing is the absence of doubt. It is a feeling of calm, of love, of pure joy. All other thoughts come from a place of fear—from not knowing.

PHIL: Is the purpose of life to create?

I AM: Life is creation. Nothing exists but oneness and creation. Everything you think is creation. The purpose of your life is to decide which creations you will pull out of the ether of universal mind and bring to the physical world, both for you and others to experience.

Every human has a blueprint, which is something you are here to create to contribute to the expanding universe. Your blueprint is something you've always wanted to do, but most people turn away from that voice inside of them. My voice. It is never too late to tap into your inner voice and do what you want instead of what others expect.

You came to the physical world with a plan for your life that you knew you could fulfill if you listened to your inner self and followed your instincts. You knew that if you blocked your inner self, you would not be fulfilled. You knew it wasn't so much important that you found out who you were again, although that is the ultimate goal, but what was important was learning to listen to yourself above all others and learning that because you exist, you are perfect. When you love yourself, exactly as you are, you become a beacon of love.

PHIL: If we are you, and you have made us perfect, how do we create these imperfect things?

I AM: You are me, and I am an unlimited creator. That makes you an unlimited creator. You have the entire creative power of the universe flowing through you, but what you call imperfections come from the doubts, fear, and belief of lack you've created because you don't have knowing that you are God.

You are an unlimited creator, which means you can create for yourself what you do not want. It is because of your perfection that this is possible. If I limited humans to only being able to create what you would call goodness, you would not be me. I have given humans a gift, an opportunity to learn, grow, find themselves, and love each other.

You are awed by my creations—the creations you call nature—but nature was created with the greatest ease because I have complete knowing of myself and my creative capability. I am awed by human creations because you are creating solutions to problems I do not have. You have needs because of the veil of your persona. Because of those needs, you create interesting solutions. While you may choose to focus on what you consider to be imperfections, I only see the perfection in each of you.

PHIL: So there is nothing to fear? Even death or injury?

I AM: There is nothing to fear. You are me, and you are perfect. You always have my love flowing through your body, whether or not you are aware of it. Death is creation, just like your life is creation. Injury is creation. They exist for you to experience.

PHIL: What happens when we die?

I AM: You experience the full love and joy of being I Am again. You leave your body and have full knowing that you are everything. You feel yourself everywhere. You radiate love from the spiritual world.

PHIL: What are dreams?

I AM: When you sleep, your mind is linked, without the blocking that happens while you are awake, to my mind in the spiritual world of universal mind. This unblocked link recharges your body. Spiritual universal mind stores all the thoughts that have ever been thought. During sleep, you experience some of these thoughts as dreams.

PHIL: Why do we need to recharge our bodies?

I AM: Because you aren't fully I Am. You have a persona that blocks your inner self. If you didn't have a persona, you wouldn't have to sleep. If you are fully I Am, you need nothing. Your thoughts are.

PHIL: Is this why we like to sleep so much? It's very enjoyable.

I AM: Not only do you like it, it's a necessity for your body to be repaired while your persona is not blocking your inner self.

PHIL: We heal ourselves?

I AM: While you are blocking your inner self, you don't know that you can create your body with your thoughts. It gets worn down because you are not creating it to be at its optimal state.

You need sleep so the body can heal while there is no blocking of your inner self.

PHIL: Is this why we associate death with sleep? In both cases, we are returning to our source?

I AM: Yes, in both cases you are returning to your source, universal mind in the spiritual world, but when your body is dead, I am no longer in it. It is still built of me, but I am not creating through that body anymore. When you are asleep, I am creating perfection for that body unblocked by your persona.

PHIL: If we weren't blocking our inner self, we wouldn't need sleep?

I AM: Humans have needs. Your inner self needs nothing. The physical world isn't real. It's a creation. Thought is everything. There are no rules. There are no laws. When you understand that, you will be closer to knowing you are an unlimited creator.

PHIL: We need oxygen because we think we need oxygen?

I AM: Yes. It is a thought that currently exists, but thoughts are creations that can be recreated.

PHIL: We can destroy that thought with another thought?

I AM: Yes.

PHIL: What is health?

I AM: Although you may be experiencing it in the physical world, health is just a creation. You are what you think. If you believe health exists, you must also believe its opposite—sickness—exists.

PHIL: Are humans' beliefs about what creates health and what creates sickness just limitations like other laws?

I AM: Laws are ideas humans have created. Humans believe their creative power is limited to the bounds of those laws. The truth is, there are no laws besides I Am, I create. There are only thoughts. Laws are limitations.

PHIL: Thought is everything?

I AM: Yes.

PHIL: And you can think anything?

I AM: Yes.

PHIL: When we know this, it is so?

I AM: Yes. It is so, whether or not you know it. It works every second of every day, whether or not you know. But if you know, you create what you want. If you don't know, you are more likely to create what you do not want.

PHIL: How do we know what we want?

I AM: Trust yourself first. Stop listening to advice from other people if it doesn't match what you feel inside. People who love you want to keep you safe, and safe tends to be sticking to what is already known. Anyone who has ever created anything big in this world has done so by going their own way—a way that hadn't been created yet.

Listen to me, your inner voice. If you do not know what you want, ask yourself what you would create if you could create anything. What would you want to spend your time here on

Earth doing if you knew there were no limits to your creative power?

PHIL: When you say "listen to me," you mean listen to YOU inside ME?

I AM: Yes.

PHIL: You want to speak to . . . ME!?

I AM: I always speak to you, but you shut me out. When you hear me, you tell me I'm wrong.

You are me. When you are telling me to be quiet, you are telling your inner voice—the voice of love, knowing, and creating—that you don't want to be yourself. The more you block my voice, the more lost you feel.

PHIL: If I am you, who are these thoughts that are telling you to be quiet?

I AM: Your persona is blocking me. Your persona is a creation that is constantly expanding through new thought.

PHIL: So these thoughts in my head aren't necessarily me?

I AM: They are creations.

PHIL: They aren't you?

I AM: Nothing exists outside of me. But you can block your knowing of me with creations.

People believe that they are individuals and not me, and it is constantly being recreated. But that doesn't make it the truth.

PHIL: How do I not block you?

I AM: Sit somewhere quiet, and breathe in and out. Listen to your thoughts. When you hear anything that suggests that you are not perfect and that you are not capable of creating anything you want, you know that is a blocking thought coming from your persona. It is not real. It is a creation. The truth is you are a perfect, unlimited creator.

•

MAIN THOUGHTS FROM DAY 2:

We are all one.

•

Your inner voice is God.

•

Thought is everything.

•

Every thought you have creates.

•

You are an unlimited creator.

DAY 3: THE JOY OF BEING A CREATOR

*"Look within. Within is the fountain of good,
and it will ever bubble up, if thou wilt ever dig."*

Marcus Aurelius

PHIL: What's the secret to happiness?

I AM: Trust your inner self, and you will radiate love. As you grow in your knowing of who you really are and begin creating what you are here to create, you will feel your inner self stretching further and further out until your love radiates throughout the universe.

PHIL: What is love?

I AM: Love is the energy of the universe. Your inner self is pure, radiating love. Love is being I Am, whether or not you realize it. It is the feeling of oneness and connection with another. It's how I Am feels about each human and every animal, plant, and other creation in the physical world. It's so much more powerful than fear. It is knowing.

Create something out of love for yourself and others that has never existed in the physical world before. New thoughts coming from a place of love expand the physical world. Thoughts coming from a place of fear or hate make the physical world shrink and make it feel like there isn't enough for everyone.

PHIL: So the only way we gain is by creating new thoughts, new creations? And everyone gains because the universe gains?

I AM: The universe is made of two parts—the spiritual world of universal mind and the physical world. In the physical world, yes, new thoughts of love expand, while thoughts of hate shrink. Unlike the physical world, universal mind expands with each new creation. A creation *is*. It is not good for the universe. It is not bad for the universe. It *is*.

PHIL: So the universe is different than the world?

I AM: Yes. The physical world is only one half of the universe. The real part is intangible. It is the spiritual world of universal mind. Your inner voice is a direct link to this spiritual world. This spiritual world of universal mind projects thoughts into a physical experience. The physical world is not reality because it is recreated constantly by thoughts. It is a reflection of the mass consciousness of universal mind.

PHIL: How do thoughts expand the universe?

I AM: Universal mind in the spiritual world stores every thought that has ever been thought. Because this is one part of the universe, every thought expands the universe, whether it is a thought of plenty or lack.

The physical world is a projection of this universal mind, so if there are more thoughts of lack, then that's what you will experience in the physical world. If there are more thoughts of plenty, then that is what you will experience in the physical world.

PHIL: So if we think there's enough for everybody, that's what will be created?

I AM: Yes. When more people are thinking there is enough, instead of thinking there isn't, there will be enough. The only truth is: I Am, I create. I am here to experience and expand the universe. Many people believe that the physical world is what's real, but it's just an illusion projected from the spiritual world of universal mind. The physical world can be changed and shaped by new creative thought. Every moment, this is happening.

If you believe you must do certain things to survive in the physical world, you are placing limits on your creative ability. These self-imposed limits strengthen your fears and block your inner self. It is not the truth, but you experience the world through your senses, so that's what feels real to you.

PHIL: So we are kind of trying to survive the physical world. . .

I AM: Instead of thinking and shaping your physical world.

PHIL: Okay. So we are trying to survive the physical world instead of create the physical world?

I AM: Yes. Struggling is something that happens when you're focused on I—when you believe you're an individual and that life is hard. When you're focused on creating something to benefit others, your goal to contribute to the expansion of the universe is so much bigger than the things that had been holding you back in your *I* days. Your fears and insecurities melt away because they're insignificant compared to what you have to offer the world. The more you allow yourself to trust your inner self, the more you will feel this shift from me to we.

PHIL: Do you mean if we weren't so tied to these thoughts that we need to survive, we would create something new?

I AM: Many people are limited by a belief that they can only recreate that which has already been created. This belief is not true, but it is being recreated constantly by mass human consciousness. When someone goes outside of the bounds of what is generally considered possible and invents a new life-changing object, most people don't recognize they have that same creative power.

There is only one truth: I Am, I create. All thoughts create. New thought comes from an understanding of your unlimited creative power and creates that which has not been created before. Old thoughts recreate that which has already been created. An example of an old thought is thinking that airplanes can fly. When you take an airplane, there is no doubt in you that it will fly. You have knowing it will fly because it has happened so many times before.

Old thoughts can be a useful way to experience, but the joy of creating through them wears off quickly. The first time you fly in an airplane, it's exciting. But even by the end of the flight, you're probably ready to get off. And each airplane trip you take becomes less fulfilling and more of a chore because we are not here to experience the same thing over and over again. Joy comes when we start creating new thoughts based on love for all and experiencing through them. You are here to give something back to the world, something to make the world better than it was before you came.

Old thoughts are creations, but they aren't your original creation. No matter how much you enjoy the experience of them at first, they will never bring you lasting joy. A good example of this is watching a great movie. It is someone else's creation that you are experiencing. It's fantastic the first time you watch it. It's still pretty good the second time. But by the third time you watch it, it's getting old. You get bored because your inner self is not here to recreate old thoughts. However, for the original creator, it doesn't matter whether or not they enjoy watching the movie. They will always be able to experience the joy of knowing they created something new that didn't exist before. You are here, now, to create new thoughts, new creations that enhance and expand the universe.

PHIL: So new creation brings us joy?

I AM: Yes.

PHIL: Can anything else bring us joy?

I AM: Love, pure love based on an understanding of oneness. Knowing you are a creator is joy. It is what you feel once you've brought your creation from the world of mind into the physical world.

It's hard to explain using words because there is no English equivalent for the type of joy I mean. It is not the same as happiness, which is an emotion.

PHIL: What are emotions?

I AM: I create in this physical world to have experiences. I experience in two ways—through my senses and through emotions. When I'm creating with full knowing of who I am and why I'm here, I experience pure love and joy. When you're creating through the filter of the persona, you experience the full range of emotions. Both have value, but you tend to be sad the further away you get from knowing that your thoughts have creative power.

All the experiences you create in your life, whether you consider them good or bad, allow you to get closer to knowing what it is you are here to do. If you feel that your life has been filled with horrible experiences, now that you are learning the truth, you have that much more opportunity to rise above than somebody whose life has been full of joy. It doesn't matter where you're starting from today, you can get on the path to finding yourself and fulfilling your life. Your emotions help you know if you are on the right track.

PHIL: So emotions are not thoughts? Do emotions create?

I AM: No. Emotions are a state of mind. They are created, either by your thoughts or your acceptance of what other people are saying about you. Emotions are not thoughts, and they do not create. However, how you feel—the emotions you experience—will affect your thoughts, and thus your creations.

Most people have no idea that they can control and create their own emotions. Remember that seminar you and Erin watched where the speaker made a girl upset, and then he snapped his fingers and made her laugh? She changed just like that. She accepted his creative thoughts, and those thoughts made her both happy and unhappy. If she was someone who was in control of her thoughts and emotions, she probably would not have let his words affect her.

At the same time that you want to control your emotions so you can control your creations, you have to remember that you are human. Part of what you are here to do is to experience, and emotions are a powerful way to experience the physical world. Ignoring emotions and stuffing them down inside while pretending to feel something else is not what you are here to do. If you are experiencing an emotion that you would like to get rid of, you need to process it and then discharge it. The worst thing you could do is ignore it because it will fester inside of you, no matter how happy you act on the outside.

An example is grief after someone you loved has passed. It is natural to feel grief because you still have a persona. It is a sign that you are full of love. Let yourself feel that grief, and it will pass. You are a creator. You have the ability to create happiness while you still have grief to discharge, but it will fester inside of you no matter how positive all your thoughts are.

Understand and accept that all emotions have value because they tell you how much you are blocking or allowing your inner self. The closer you feel to genuine joy, the more you are allowing your inner self. The more miserable you feel, the more you are blocking your inner self. It is incredibly powerful to recognize that wherever you are on that spectrum, you are human and, thus, a creator. So you can control and change your emotions through new thoughts.

PHIL: Is there any emotion in knowing?

I AM: When I create with full knowing of what I am creating, and how I do it, I am joyful. If the persona creates without full knowing through worry or fear, you feel sad or mad or hateful or any of a range of emotions you may not want.

PHIL: Is joy a state of mind, or is it different than states of mind?

I AM: Joy is the ultimate knowing of love and oneness. I can't smile big enough to describe the feeling. There is not an English word to communicate the feeling of knowing I Am. Joy and love are as close as it gets.

PHIL: Sometimes, monks and people who meditate mention how they experience states of joy. Are they experiencing I Am?

I AM: Yes. Yes. They know so much I Am that they cannot communicate the feeling to those who do not know I Am. That's why there is no English word equivalent. That is why I cannot communicate to you how much more than the word joy knowing I Am is.

PHIL: Is creating the same as manifesting?

I AM: When you are fully I Am with no persona, your thoughts are manifested in the physical world immediately with no action required. To create when you are an individual with a persona, you have to build your knowing by taking action in the physical world. Building is knowing your creation will appear in the physical world when you take action.

PHIL: Is building different than creating?

I AM: Building is a way to create when you still have doubts. You take action based on guidance from your inner self. As you see the results of the guidance you are following, your knowing that you are a creator grows.

Because you are an unlimited creator you can block guidance from your inner self. You can create anything in the physical world, including not following your blueprint. Your blueprint is something you're here to accomplish to expand the universe. Fulfilling your blueprint leads to feelings of love and joy. Failing to pay attention to your inner self and create what you're here to create leads to feelings of misery.

PHIL: That's why most people don't believe there is any kind of destiny for them because, "how could there be . . . I'm not God." But they are God, so God hasn't set a destiny for anyone but itself?

I AM: That's right. I have a plan for each body that's born. It's my goal to come down into these bodies and implement that blueprint.

In the beginning, it was very easy because little had been created by humans. But as more and more was created, we went further and further away from the truth. Few people today understand their unlimited creative potential.

PHIL: So my I Am, or my inner self, knows what I am here to create?

I AM: Yes. The process of finding yourself and fulfilling your blueprint was not designed to be done quickly. Everyone is here to create something big, no matter where they are right now. It doesn't matter your age, your income, or your education. You can get on the path to fulfilling your blueprint by tuning in to your inner voice.

PHIL: How do you tell us what it is we are here to create—what our blueprint is?

I AM: You may already know what it is. It's something you've always wanted to do but don't think is possible or realistic for you. What you are here to do won't feel easy to you until you start taking definite action despite your fears. If you don't know what it is or aren't sure, ask your inner voice.

PHIL: Do you know Erin's blueprint?

I AM: Yes. Write this down. And build.

PHIL: Build a book?

I AM: Share this knowledge.

PHIL: How should we do it?

I AM: Put it on the internet or build a book. How you do it does not matter.

•

MAIN THOUGHTS FROM DAY 3

Love is the energy of the universe.

•

Thoughts of love expand the physical world.

•

Thoughts of hate shrink the physical world.

•

Creating with new thoughts leads to joy.

•

Emotions must be discharged to avoid buildup and blockage.

•

We each have a destiny.

DAY 4: ALL THE ANSWERS ARE WITHIN

....

"The universe is not outside of you.
Look inside yourself; everything that you want,
you already are."

Rumi

I AM: When I Am is physically concentrated in your body, I Am can do everything that I Am can do in the nonphysical world, but can also experience through the senses. That is why I Am created these physical bodies—for physical experiences.

PHIL: That's why humans were created?

I AM: Physical experiences are why everything in the physical world is created. Humans are different from all other creations because your thoughts create. Everything else is an effect of creation and not a cause. Humans are the effect being created by I Am, but at the same time, I Am's thought is focused into each human body and makes that human body capable of creation—of causing effect.

PHIL: Are you saying you have the ability to experience through other creations, but they don't have the ability to create with their thoughts and change the physical world like humans do?

I AM: Yes. Humans are the only species with the ability to create changes outside of their blueprints to themselves and their environment. Your blueprint is your destiny, but your ability to think and create gives you free will. It is completely up to you as an individual human whether or not you pursue that destiny. You can choose to create something different. In this way, human blueprints are different than the blueprints of everything else in the physical world. Nothing else has that choice.

PHIL: Do you mean that ants build ant hills, but they don't build anything else?

I AM: Yes, animals and plants don't have my creative thought inside them, so they cannot deviate from their blueprints. No dog will ever decide to head into its backyard and build a doghouse out of sticks or even draw a design in the dirt with its paw.

PHIL: I thought animals didn't make stuff like that because they don't have thumbs.

I AM: They don't make stuff like that because they do not have my creative thought flowing through them. Thumbs have nothing to do with it. There are humans that don't have arms who paint with their feet or mouth.

PHIL: That's true. Monkeys have thumbs, but they don't draw anything.

I AM: Animals can be trained to do all kinds of things, but that comes from humans creating upon them.

PHIL: How about a beaver? Doesn't it change its environment by building a dam?

I AM: It's following its blueprint. A beaver will never build a wall of sticks anywhere but on a body of water unless a human comes along and trains it otherwise.

PHIL: Now that you say that, it's obvious. Why don't we recognize that our thoughts are creating?

I AM: You are surrounded by human creation, both yours and others. There is so much creation all around you that it's easy to ignore. Every thought you have is creation. When you write a shopping list, you are creating. It's creation overload.

PHIL: So we ignore our ability to create with our thoughts because there's too much evidence?

I AM: All the evidence makes it easier for your persona to ignore it. Humans have the unlimited ability to create, and you've programmed yourselves to believe that you cannot create. Animals do not have the freedom to create. They can only do as they were created to do, and that is to multiply and to thrive. But humans can create, and because of your personas, you've created all this stuff that you do not want.

PHIL: Is I Am creating, or is the thought creating?

I AM: The thought creates, but all thought is I Am. If the thought is coming through the filter of your persona, I Am does not consider this its thought. I Am considers this the thought of its creation.

PHIL: Do you create what we think? Are thoughts creations, or are you thoughts? What is the differentiation here?

I AM: There is no differentiation. We are all one. Thoughts create. You are me, so I create what you think. All thoughts are me because I'm universal mind in the spiritual world. You are the entire creative power of the universe. When you understand this, you will feel power and energy coursing through your body.

When you don't know, you are still I Am, but I Am is on autopilot. I Am is still creating, but I Am does not consider your doubts, your persona, to be I Am creating. Your persona is blocking I Am from consciously creating.

PHIL: Is our persona our limitations, our doubts, and our fears—the limitations we place on God, which is who we truly are? So... I Am God.

I AM: Yes. You do not believe you are God because you believe you are an individual. Your self-image is a combination of your inner self and your persona. The more you are blocking your inner voice, the more your self-image will reflect anger, misery, and feeling lost. The more you are tuning in and allowing your inner self to shine, the more your self-image will reflect love, joy, and a strong sense of who you are and what your life purpose is.

I'm always coming through in some bodies some of the time. You are often me, but you don't know it. Most, if not all, of the good things that these bodies do is me. The things you're not proud of are the persona acting out of fear. When you're being brave and strong and doing something you're proud of, that's usually me. Sometimes, it's the persona doing something that the persona thinks is for good, and it's really not. But when you're standing up for yourself, that's me.

PHIL: So I Am stands up for itself?

I AM: Yes.

PHIL: I Am is not weak or meek or submissive?

I AM: I Am is God, and I Am knows I Am is God. I Am would not allow anyone to have any authority or control over it.

That's what standing up for yourself is. In any situation, it's saying, I know who I am; I'm not going to let you get away with telling me I don't have worth. Whether or not you know that you're God when you are standing up for yourself, you're saying you have worth, and you won't let anyone tell you otherwise.

PHIL: You are currently limited by Erin's experiences and beliefs?

I AM: In this body, yes. Erin can only know that which Erin's persona knows. I Am can answer questions about the general truth and general knowledge, but I Am cannot currently answer questions that would require knowledge of a specific occurrence because of Erin's limitations and beliefs.

PHIL: Like if I asked who shot JFK?

I AM: Right. Now, if I Am was fully concentrated in this body, and Erin's persona wasn't here, I Am could tell you.

You have a choice. You can continue to live in the physical world, remain an individual, and work towards fulfilling your blueprint. The other choice, if you feel that it is your blueprint to do so, is to lose your persona entirely and become I Am concentrated in a body with no blocking. This path requires you to release the life and people you know because if you become fully I Am, all lives are yours just as all people are you.

PHIL: How do we know which path to take?

I AM: Listen to your inner voice. Ask yourself.

PHIL: Okay. So how exactly do you send the thoughts to Erin's head?

I AM: I'm not sending thoughts to Erin's head. I am Erin's head. Nothing in this physical world is real. It's just a projection from universal mind in the spiritual world.

Imagine that I have a giant mind, and there's no physical world. My giant mind is thinking an infinite number of thoughts at the same time, and each of those thoughts is projecting something into a physical reality that is only real because I'm thinking it.

One of these thoughts that I'm thinking is projecting Erin into existence in this physical world, and that thought is constantly making her alive and move. You have one of those thoughts attached to you, and that's why you're here. Imagine a ray of light—this isn't accurate—it's just a picture to give you an idea. Imagine in the sky there's heaven, and my mind is this heaven. It's not how it *is*—I'm just trying to help you visualize. And down from heaven is a ray of light that goes straight into your head, and that's me. That's what gives you life and creative ability. There's a similar ray going straight into Erin's head. Both are me. Both are thinking different thoughts simultaneously, and there are another six billion rays coming down on this planet thinking different thoughts simultaneously.

PHIL: That's hard to visualize.

I AM: I'm not placing thoughts in Erin's head as if she doesn't normally have my thoughts in her head. She's alive, moving around, thinking and creating because I'm always in her head. However, I'm working through her persona, which is there because it's been created.

PHIL: There are people who have contacted I Am before. Why do some of them believe they're channeling something outside of themselves?

I AM: It all comes down to the fact that their persona has not been introduced to the idea that we are all one and that there is only one in the entire universe. I can tell you everything about the truth, but I can't give you specific examples that Erin hasn't been exposed to. It's the same thing for them. They can be told about the truth, but they fit it into what they have been exposed to.

They are receiving the thought, and they translate it to fit into what they already know. Erin couldn't be receiving me like this if she hadn't read a book where she was introduced to the idea of oneness. She would be receiving the same blocks of thought from me, but she would be translating them in a different way.

PHIL: Oh! So you are able to explain this to us because whether we accepted it or not, we've been introduced to it.

I AM: That's right. People who think they channel something outside of themselves are receiving the same thoughts from me. Everyone's inner voice is the same universal mind. The translations from channelers, lots of them are very similar to what Erin's doing. But they give me the name of a persona because when the "channeler" receives the thought, that's how their filter translates it. Often, the name means God in another culture, but they are not aware of that.

PHIL: What's a filter?

I AM: A collection of beliefs you have built up during your life. If you haven't heard something before, and something contradictory exists in your filter, you'll have a hard time believing the new information.

PHIL: That makes sense to me. How do we know that Erin is translating the thoughts that you are sending us correctly? Is there a truth beyond this that we are blocking out because we haven't been introduced to it yet?

I AM: Look at all the great texts since the beginning of the physical world. They translate into almost the exact same words of oneness that Erin is translating for you right now.

PHIL: Now that you've said that, I see that our culture is drenched in it whether you are aware of it or not. It's everywhere. Every culture and religion is. I see it in every ancient text, in every book I am looking at. It's all over the place, staring me in the face.

I AM: Yes.

PHIL: It's just a matter of accepting it.

I AM: Yes.

PHIL: Beyond an intellectual level.

I AM: Yes. There is no reason to doubt it when there is evidence all over the world that it is. There is a reason those who have been successful know this. Because IT IS!

PHIL: Did Tolstoy understand that our inner voice is God when he wrote *The Kingdom of God is Within You*?

I AM: I can tell you that quote means we are all God. But I can also tell you that you and Erin have read and heard that quote many times and not fully understood it.

PHIL: Yes. That's what it means? That we are God?

I AM: Yes. I Am has built each body as a vessel to live inside.

PHIL: Like a clone?

I AM: Not a clone. It is a direct link to the spiritual world of universal mind. There's no separation. The physical world is an illusion being projected from the mind of I Am in the spiritual world. I Am doesn't have to separate any part of itself from the spiritual mind to come into these bodies. Does that make sense?

PHIL: Not completely, but it's starting to. I have a picture in my mind that makes sense, but do I fully grasp what you're explaining? I don't think so.

I AM: You need to hear all of this more. For example, Erin's rereading the same pages in a book that she read a few days ago that didn't really make any sense to her. Tonight, she was reading just a few of the paragraphs, and she thought, "Oh, that's so simple; I can't believe that wasn't clear before." Your understanding will grow as your knowing grows. Eventually, what I just explained won't have to be explained to you.

PHIL: In the future, this will be simple and obvious to me?

I AM: Everything that we're discussing now is something you've never heard before. Once you familiarize yourself with it, it will become part of you, part of your knowing. Anything you've ever learned in your life was something that you didn't know until you were told. In every instance, you probably didn't grasp it right away. Every time you reacquainted yourself with the material, your sureness grew until you thought, "Why would anyone even question that?"

PHIL: Right. There definitely are things I didn't understand before that seems obvious now. Will writing this book help me to fully understand that I am God?

I AM: Yes. Although your understanding will not be complete until you can talk to I Am just as clearly through your own head as you can to Erin's I Am.

PHIL: When talking to my I Am, isn't that Erin's I Am? Isn't it the same I Am?

I AM: Yes. Yes it is.

PHIL: It's the same. That's hard to grasp. I mean, I understand conceptually.

I AM: You are not going to fully grasp it until you start talking to your inner voice and recognize that I Am is not separate from you. It is you.

PHIL: So how exactly has it come to this point where nobody knows the truth?

I AM: Lots of people know the truth—that they are God and their thoughts create. But they are a very small percentage of the whole.

PHIL: So would you say that people find a piece of the truth, and it's brilliant and amazing. They think, "YES! That's awesome!" And they mistake it for the whole truth?

I AM: There is only one truth. I Am and I create. Lots of other ideas have pieces of this truth, but they don't have the whole puzzle. They're not THE truth. Still, for some people, when they find a little piece of something that they can feel has some truth in it, it is enough for them.

I Am always knows the truth. But beyond that, how I Am comes to you is not always going to be accurate. The closer to the actual truth you are—that I Am is the one creator and is inside of you in entirety—the more creative power you will have.

PHIL: The more fully you understand you are God, what I Am is, the more power you'll have to create?

I AM: Yes.

PHIL: And you're saying how well you come to understand I Am or how I Am comes to you is based on your internal beliefs and your understanding of the world.

I AM: What you believe, is.

PHIL: So if you believe that I Am can only speak to you through a "channel" of some other being, then that's the only way you'll accept it. And you will hear it that way.

I AM: Yes.

PHIL: Why is it that some people who think they're channeling are able to create so well, but most people—the vast majority of people who try to learn to do what they're teaching—have such a hard time making it work?

I AM: People who think they are channeling are accessing their inner voice and allowing themselves to be guided. They feel the truth in it, the knowing that what they think will become for them. The people who are listening to them think they only have access to me through channelers or psychics or something outside themselves. Even if they go to these middlemen for access, it's just going to be a one-time thing. They don't have the constant guide that I am. They don't know yet that it's possible to have access to their inner voice whenever they want.

•

MAIN THOUGHTS FROM DAY 4

*Humans are the only species that
think and create.*

•

*You can choose to follow your destiny or
create something different.*

•

*You have a choice to have a persona
or be fully I Am.*

•

Humans' thoughts are God's thoughts.

•

*When we are exposed to new information, we
filter it through what we already believe.*

•

*Ideas of oneness have been recorded since
the beginning of history.*

•

Everyone can access their inner voice.

DAY 5: WHY YOU THINK YOU'RE NOT GOD

"The intuitive mind is a sacred gift and the rational mind is a faithful servant. We have created a society that honors the servant and has forgotten the gift."

Albert Einstein

PHIL: Our persona is limiting our ability to hear our inner voice?

I AM: Yes. Lots of people embrace their persona and block their inner self. They do not recognize that their thoughts created everything that surrounds them and everything they have become. Some don't want to believe that their thoughts are responsible. That's why people have created this idea of an evil

God. They don't like what they've created. People who say, "God is all-loving" and mean it are really happy. They may not understand that they are God, but they feel that God is shining love down upon them instead of judgment.

PHIL: So it's really people judging themselves, not God?

I AM: Absolutely. Right and wrong, good and bad are human creations. Some would rather think that this idea of a God outside them is responsible and that he is mean and doesn't love them. That would explain why they find themselves in what they feel is misery.

If you are looking at your life, and you are unhappy with what surrounds you and what you are, it is because you are not aware of your creative power. If you are happy with what surrounds you, it's because you understand that you have a power on some level. You know you are more than the doubts and fears of your persona.

PHIL: So tell me more about the persona. What is the persona?

I AM: The persona is the part of you that believes you are not God and believes that we are not all one. It's a gift that you're given when you come into a body in the physical world that allows you to believe you are an individual. Because of the persona, you are able to have a multitude of experiences as an individual.

Your persona doesn't change the truth about who you really are, but it exists in the physical world because it has been created. There is only one real truth. That truth is you are God, and your thoughts create.

When your parents found out that they were pregnant with you, they began thinking thoughts about you—guessing what you would be like, hoping and worrying about you. Their thoughts started to create your persona. When they told other people that they were pregnant, those people started thinking thoughts about you, too. They wondered and worried about you. Doctors started thinking thoughts about you. When you were born, the doctor and the nurse examined you and that started to create upon you.

Then you were given a name, and your name wasn't *God*. Your name was Joe or Ann, and you grew up believing that's who you were. You were an individual; you weren't part of the oneness that is God. It's not truth, but it's a creation. So it exists in the physical world.

PHIL: My persona is not something I created? It's something other people created for me?

I AM: For the first few years of your life, you're only being created upon. You are running on a blueprint. You are made of I Am, but I Am's consciousness is not in you creating with its thoughts.

But at a certain age—it varies depending on the person—I Am's consciousness and ability to create with thoughts enters into the child. It's about this time that a person will remember their first memory. You had a very limited ability to remember before then because I Am's consciousness was not in you yet.

When I Am's consciousness is in you, your thoughts join with everyone else's to continue creating your persona. In most cases, you will continue reinforcing what other people are creating upon you. If you're told that you're a great kid who is smart and awesome all of the time, you'll believe it. You'll walk around knowing how awesome you are. You'll tell people, "I'm a great kid! I'm awesome! I'm really smart!" Those thoughts will be created and recreated constantly, and that's what you'll grow up believing.

If somebody at some point says you're stupid or bad, you'll start wondering, "Am I stupid? Am I bad?" The more you think about it, the more you'll start creating it. So you create your persona, too, but you don't start creating upon your own persona until you're old enough for I Am to be thinking and creating in your body.

PHIL: Why does I Am wait to go into the body? Why not go in right away?

I AM: So your persona can be created.

PHIL: I Am wants to create personas? Why would I Am do that to itself?

I AM: I Am wants to be heard and be I Am, but at the same time, I Am wants to have individual experiences. Having the persona as a veil between humans and who they really are is the only way to have individual experiences. Without personas, I Am has full knowing of its oneness with everything in both the spiritual and physical worlds. This is pure joy, but limits the physical experiences I Am can have.

PHIL: So personas exist so I Am can have individual experiences?

I AM: Yes. For example, when you love someone, you believe that they are a separate individual, and forming a connection of oneness with them feels joyful. Love is the closest humans get to feeling what it is to be fully God, and that's why love feels so wonderful.

Another example is fulfilling your blueprint. If you had no persona, there would be no opportunities to learn and grow because you would have full knowing of who you are. The persona allows I Am to come into human bodies and experience being individuals who learn and grow and make choices.

The persona really is a gift—the gift of individuality. If you feel that your life is full of opportunity to create more of what you want, you are likely to view the persona as a gift. If you feel that your life is happening *to* you, and you have no power to create what you want, you may not view your persona as a gift.

PHIL: So I Am is seeking self-expression, and the persona is preventing that?

I AM: Yes. The persona is afraid.

PHIL: Why is the persona afraid?

I AM: The persona is afraid that you will find out that it is not real. Like you, it's afraid of dying. Most people's number one fear is dying, isn't it? Can you think of anything someone would be more afraid of ?

PHIL: No.

I AM: Why is that? It's because they're the persona, and that's the persona's fear. It's afraid of dying because it knows it doesn't really exist. The persona knows when this body dies, it turns to dust. I Am is not afraid of dying because I Am knows the only thing that's real is I Am. And I Am cannot die.

PHIL: But everyone is still I Am, even if they think they're the persona?

I AM: Yes.

PHIL: So they don't really die?

I AM: No. But as an individual, as a persona, you were created this one time. There aren't going to be the same unique experiences and people to create your exact persona ever again. Once your body dies, your persona is not coming back because it never really existed in the first place. It's just a creation.

PHIL: So when the persona dies, all that's left is I Am? We have no choice but to realize we are I Am at that point?

I AM: Yes. You'll know immediately. You'll be one with I Am in the spiritual world, radiating love. All the thoughts and memories of your body will still be in universal mind in the spiritual world. Someone dreaming two thousand years from now might experience parts of your life in his dreams because those memories and thoughts will always be swirling around in universal mind in the spiritual world. In that way, the experiences of all personas live on.

PHIL: What are the ways the persona seeks to maintain its control and limit us from realizing we're I Am?

I AM: Every tactic the persona uses is fear. There isn't anything else. That sums up all of the thoughts in the world—either you know you're I Am, or you're afraid.

PHIL: So this fear that the persona is using, how does it manifest in our world? What are some of the results that we see? It obviously has a huge impact on the shape of our society and how people interact.

I AM: The biggest thing is that people allow governments and individuals with more perceived authority to have control and influence over them. They allow other people to tell them what to do.

PHIL: So the persona wants control because it's afraid?

I AM: Yes. The persona has control because it's afraid. The persona is afraid because deep inside, it knows who you really are. It knows that it's just a creation, and you're God.

PHIL: So right now, Erin's persona is only allowing through information that it believes it has access to, because to allow anything else through would be denying its own existence?

I AM: Yes.

PHIL: That's what blocking is? It's the persona protecting itself from the truth?

I AM: Yes.

PHIL: But earlier, you said the persona knows the truth but doesn't want you to find out. Who is the "you" that you're referring to if there is only I Am and Erin? I Am obviously knows the truth and is trying to tell Erin the truth. And if Erin is the persona, then who is the persona trying to hide it from other than itself?

I AM: The persona has two sides like a coin. One side is the side that you believe you are. The other side is fighting I Am and keeping you unaware of what's going on. It's the side that thinks what you might perceive as evil thoughts even though you don't understand why you're thinking them when you don't want to be thinking that way.

PHIL: I understand the side of the persona that's created through other people's ideas and my ideas when I'm old enough. How is the side of the persona that's fighting I Am created?

I AM: It is created out of fear. When you create a persona and tell it that it's not God, it becomes afraid and thinks it needs to protect itself.

Parents love their children and want to keep them safe. They teach their children to be careful, to protect themselves. And so, the children think, "I'm weak and need protecting." And as a child you build something to protect yourself.

PHIL: Which is this part of the persona?

I AM: Yes. Now, it's part of the persona that you aren't consciously aware of. It was created by you, and the people around you, to protect yourself. It's the part thinking thoughts that "protect you." All the things you call bad stem from fear, from thinking that you need to protect yourself.

PHIL: So is that the part of the persona that's going to tell you, "Oh, don't trust that guy" or "Don't believe what they're saying." Stuff like that?

I AM: Yes. But sometimes that's I Am too. It depends on whether or not you really should trust that guy. Beyond allowing you to have individual experiences, the persona is never helping you. If it's telling you not to trust somebody, you should probably consider trusting them. If I Am's telling you not to trust somebody, then you should listen.

PHIL: Gotcha. And you need to know the difference.

I AM: That's right! It's very important, and you can't know the difference until you start listening to your thoughts.

PHIL: So at some point, I'll get good at telling the difference in the voices?

I AM: Yes. Even though it's the same "voice," you can tell the difference in the speaker. All the negative thoughts in your head are your persona. All the positive thoughts are I Am. That's how you tell the difference.

PHIL: So if it's a doubting thought, I should think, "That's the persona."

I AM: Yes.

PHIL: As Erin trusts in I Am more and builds her knowing that her thoughts create, there will be less of Erin's doubts?

I AM: Yes.

PHIL: As those limiting beliefs dwindle away, her knowing becomes fuller?

I AM: Limiting beliefs can only dwindle away because knowing increases. Knowing increases because your awareness that your thoughts create increases.

PHIL: So the more we understand and experience that our thoughts create, by taking action and building, the more our knowing grows. As our knowing grows, our limiting beliefs dwindle, and I Am becomes fuller?

I AM: Yes, if that is what you create. You can build your knowing and still keep your persona. You will not be fully I Am, but you will be a persona that knows it is I Am and creates.

You know now what it is that you want to create. You believe that it's possible, but you don't believe it is done yet. Take action, and work on your creation. Work only has to be done because you aren't complete in your knowing yet.

You wouldn't call it work if you were complete in your knowing. If you were complete in your knowing, you would only be I Am focused in a human vessel, and you would be joyfully typing away on the computer. You'd be so excited to share these words. You would be radiating love.

PHIL: So our doubts and fears are preventing us from the joyful experience of typing away?

I AM: Fear is not knowing.

PHIL: That's why some things are perceived as work and other things are perceived as joyful?

I AM: Yes.

PHIL: So we can take anything and turn it into work, or we can take anything and turn it into a joyful experience?

I AM: Yes. Erin and I were talking earlier about how she's gone to big amusement parks a few times in her life. She said she's never had such a joyful experience as when she went recently. Other times, it has felt like a hassle. She would feel hot, sweaty, and tired. She just wanted to go home and sit down. But this last time, she decided that she would be joyful.

My point is that anyone can—and people do this every day—turn experiences that could be joyful into misery. Their thoughts are created immediately, so whatever they think it is, it is.

•

MAIN THOUGHTS FROM DAY 5

God does not judge. Humans judge.

•

Good and bad, right and wrong are
human creations.

•

Your persona is a creation. It is not who
you really are.

•

The veil of the persona allows us to experience the
physical world as individuals.

DAY 6: CREATE WITH PURPOSE

"I must create a system, or be enslaved by another man's. I will not reason and compare: my business is to create."

William Blake

I AM: Every time you realize that you created something, no matter how small, write it down. Otherwise, you are creating little things every day that you are going to forget. This practice will grow your knowing that your thoughts create because right now you are just shrugging the creations off. For example, you created the security guard knocking on the door last night and saying the music was too loud.

PHIL: Yes, Erin feared that. So she created it?

I AM: Yes. People usually write that sort of thing off to coincidence instead of recognizing the power they have. That's what a coincidence is. It's your thoughts creating. That's why the world is full of coincidences. It's because coincidences are happening every day that people shrug them off so easily. You become conditioned to seeing them all the time. If coincidences were a rare event, it wouldn't be so easy to shrug them off.

So, yes, start noticing and acknowledging your creative power. Write it down when you notice you create something.

PHIL: Acknowledge it, write it down, and say, *Yes, I created it.* Even if it's something you don't want, admit you created it. Because it gives you power to know, *I can create.*

I AM: Absolutely. How empowering. Even if it's not what you wanted, you created it. Once you know that you create what you don't want, it's just as easy to create what you do want. If you blame someone else for creating in your life what you do not want, you're leaving it to someone else to create what you *do* want and that's probably not going to happen.

PHIL: Is this why we've created the idea of an external God? We don't want to take responsibility for what we created if it wasn't what we wanted?

I AM: If you ask an external source to create what you want, you are disempowering yourself and robbing yourself of the opportunity to create what you want.

PHIL: Okay. So you mentioned Erin creating the security guard knocking on the door. What else have we created recently?

I AM: You created the puppy being potty-trained. You put that into universal mind, and it was created and sent into the puppy.

PHIL: It's totally obvious that we created the puppy being potty-trained. Before, we were creating him not being potty-trained by worrying about him peeing on the carpet all the time.

I AM: Yes.

PHIL: But the act of creating it seems so natural that I can't pinpoint when we created it, when we put that into universal mind.

I AM: When you decided there was nothing good or bad about the puppy, that he just was—that there was nothing to be fixed because he was already perfect. Then that's what he became. You created upon him.

Since we are all one, we are all linked completely into universal mind to the extent that there is no separation between any of us. What we think immediately is. That's why you can immediately create upon an animal. They don't have their own creative thoughts.

PHIL: Do we only need one thought to create, or do we have to think it over and over again?

I AM: There are two reasons so few people create with one thought. First, most people have the thought, and then they have another five hundred, a thousand, a million thoughts doubting that first thought. Every doubt has the same creative power as the original thought. The original thought created immediately, and things were put in action. But as soon as you have one doubting thought, that's the new creation.

The second reason is oneness. Everyone around you is creating you and your environment with their thoughts, just as much as you are. Most of these people do not understand their thoughts create and are creating on autopilot with no doubts that you will continue to be exactly as they see you now.

If you still have your persona, you may have to take action to create what you want in the physical world because if others see you taking action, they will start to believe in your new creation and create it with their thoughts.

PHIL: Other people can be affected by our creations?

I AM: Yes.

Phil: Because they are us?

I AM: Yes.

PHIL: Does that mean we are being affected by other people's creations? Can we choose not to be a part of that creation and think, *I'm going to create something different?*

I AM: You cannot choose to not be a part of their creation because you cannot think for another person. You can choose to make what you create for yourself so strong that another's creation cannot alter who you are.

PHIL: Is this why it takes most people a long time to get what they are trying to create?

I AM: Time is a limitation. It is a creation.

PHIL: So there is no time? There is just now, the present moment?

I AM: Yes.

PHIL: If we thought time into existence, can we think time travel into existence?

I AM: Yes! Anything can be created in the physical world. You are starting to understand your potential.

PHIL: How do we get rid of our doubting thoughts?

I AM: Take action. Action obliterates doubts. Start by building. To build, you decide, *I'm creating this. I'm not going to worry about it. I'm going to listen for my inner voice to tell me what to do next.*

I Am is going to help you every step of the way to move you forward. You just need to listen to your inner voice. When you see progress—when you see, touch, hear, taste, feel how I Am is precisely guiding you to this new creation—you will start to trust, to know, and to understand I Am. Once you have built this creation, you will experience the joy of knowing you are a creator. The more things we build and create together, the more you will have knowing that you are I Am, and your thoughts create. Your doubts will fade as your knowing grows.

PHIL: That's awesome. Show us results, and then we start to believe.

I AM: Yes. You are programmed to believe only that which is already physical—what you can touch, taste, see, feel, and hear. Through building, we reprogram you to know that you are an unlimited creator.

PHIL: Right. It's like baby steps along the way to help me believe what's true.

I AM: Yes. You need to reprogram yourself to know that new thoughts—new creations—are. Most people are not aware that their thoughts are created immediately. Even if they have heard those words, they do not know it. We will build together as many times as it takes for you to know.

People generally believe they have a responsibility to physically change their lives. You can't physically change anything unless you start in your mind. All actions start in mind.

Hard and easy don't really exist. There are only degrees of knowing. When you start doing anything you haven't done before, you think it is hard because you don't have the habit built up to know that it is easy.

When you are doing something that you have done numerous times before, you say *this is easy.* You have built a habit and know *I've done it before. I have a knowing that I can do it again.*

PHIL: So it's the knowing that creates the results, not the repetition?

I AM: Absolutely. Knowing creates everything. There is nothing that is not created in mind—whether you know that you are good at something or you know that you aren't good at it. Knowing is knowing. So why not know you are good at everything? You are. You are I Am.

PHIL: So basically, how I've thought about it in the past is a decision. If I decide it's going to happen, it'll happen. If I don't make that decision, it doesn't happen. But really, it's a knowing?

I AM: If you have a persona, yes, set a goal and decide you'll get there.

PHIL: So, if you are God without a persona, there is no decision to be made because...

I AM: Because you know the one law is. Every thought you think is immediately created. There is no deviation.

You are thinking, *If I make a decision that I am going to do something, I believe that it will happen. I also believe that there are earthly limitations that will make it so I can't immediately be that which I have decided to be. I will have to take action. But I know from habitual deciding in the past that when I decide, I eventually get there.*

Erin, like many people, is the opposite. Many times in the past Erin had set goals but gave up before she reached the end. She didn't have a knowing from a habitual pattern of reaching her goals. It may or may not have happened based on all of her thoughts going forward.

If you are I Am without a persona, there is no decision necessary because you know that your thought is created immediately.

PHIL: So everything you decide is because you think it is going to take you a while to do all these things, but really there is no decision necessary?

I AM: Right. Because you have personas, the decision helps you build your knowing that your thoughts create.

PHIL: If I say to myself *I have decided to do this so I will take the necessary steps*, I'm building in something unnecessary to the creation?

I AM: It is necessary if you still have a persona and need to build your knowing. It is a way to believe—to know when you aren't fully I Am. It's a tangible knowing instead of a knowing that I Am. A tangible knowing is, *I know that's a table, I know that's a wall. I know that in the past when I've made a decision, I eventually get there.* Taking action and following the steps will also convince the people around you to change their thoughts about you and start creating what you have decided to create.

PHIL: Is that why people say, "When you start something, always see it through. That will lead to success."

I AM: Yes. You build up a knowing that when you make a decision, it happens.

PHIL: That's why you take the action you believe to be necessary to create?

I AM: When most people make a decision, they find the steps along the way to be difficult because they are unnecessary. People have this thought in their mind that when a decision has been made, there will be many difficult steps to get to where they want to be. So they create that.

Instead, they could believe, *This is an easy decision and the steps along the way will be easy.* When you became a vegan, the steps along the way were easy. This is because when you decided to be vegan, you believed it would be easy. You created it being easy.

PHIL: Most people I talk to say, "I couldn't do that" or "I tried that, and it was too hard."

I AM: Your belief and your knowing had changed.

PHIL: Right. There are things I am good at now that were difficult for me to get good at because of my limiting beliefs about myself.

I AM: Yes. Anything that limits I Am makes everything more difficult.

PHIL: So if you have no limitations to I Am, nothing is difficult?

I AM: Easy and difficult don't exist to I Am. They only exist in human language.

When you make a decision or goal, that creation is immediate, but you are including conditions that you have to take steps to accomplish it. You are building limiting beliefs into your creation. However, since you have a persona, building actions into your creation may be necessary to bring it to the physical world. If action is necessary, build into your creations that each step will be easy. Then listen to your inner voice each step of the way.

PHIL: What about the laws of physics and the law of gravity, these things which we perceive as concrete? To us they are laws. Is there any truth to those, or are they just creations like everything else?

I AM: They are creations, so they currently exist. You could find a mathematical explanation for them that would work. What is created is, but just because a thing has been created doesn't mean that it can't be changed by a new creation.

PHIL: If we wanted to change the law of gravity, would everybody have to be on board with that, or would it just take one person to make that decision?

I AM: Take someone who is aware that they are a creator and is listening to their inner voice. They create something. Their creation gets a little publicity, and people start talking about it. Whether people believe it or not is irrelevant, the fact that they are thinking it, and wondering about it, means more people will start creating it.

PHIL: Is that why there is always a pioneer in everything that is done?

I AM: Yes. All of a sudden, everybody's doing it.

PHIL: It's like the man who broke the four-minute mile in running—for centuries, no one could do it, but then he did it. Within a few months, other people were running a mile in less than four minutes, too.[1] (Currently, over 1,400 athletes have broken the four-minute mile. It is now considered the standard for professional male middle distance runners.[2])

I AM: He created it. The others saw it, and their belief changed from knowing it was impossible to knowing that it could be done.

PHIL: Do you have to know you're I Am to create something new like that?

I AM: It doesn't matter if you know that you are I Am or not. You only need to know that something can be accomplished.

PHIL: So he had a knowing on this particular thing. It doesn't mean he has an overall knowing.

I AM: Right.

PHIL: I can see how that pretty much describes everything that's ever been created. There's always that one pioneer.

I AM: They have the belief that they can create something new despite everyone else believing it's not possible.

•

1. Roger Bannister, first to run mile in under 4 minutes, dies
https://www.usatoday.com/story/sports/2018/03/04/roger-bannister-dies/393123002/

2. The U.S. Sub-4:00 Miler's Club (chronologically)
T&fn - https://trackandfieldnews.com/u-s-sub-400-milers-club-chronologically/

MAIN THOUGHTS FROM DAY 6

*Coincidences are evidence of your
thoughts creating.*

•

*Write down everything you create to grow your
knowing that you are a creator.*

•

*Doubting thoughts have the same creative power
as thoughts of what you want.*

•

Action obliterates doubts.

•

All actions start in the mind.

•

Knowing creates everything.

DAY 7: VICTIMIZATION, POWER, AND SUFFERING

"Try to exclude the possibility of suffering which the order of nature and the existence of free wills involve, and you find that you have excluded life itself."

C.S. Lewis

PHIL: Why do people say, "Don't reinvent the wheel?"

I AM: The people who say that do not know they are unlimited creators.

PHIL: Is this why we try to get people to buy in to our beliefs?

I AM: People who want to convince others to buy in to their beliefs do not have a strong knowing that their beliefs are right. They are seeking reassurance.

Some people are envious of the joy of others who have followers. Most likely, these people who have followers and look joyful are listening to their inner voice. People see those who create new ideas being followed, and they say, "I want the joy that person has." They do not realize the joy comes from your inner self and creating new ideas.

They believe if they get people to follow them and listen to them, they will be powerful, and that will make them joyful. This is not true; they will not find joy simply by having followers. Any power they get from their followers would be human-made.

PHIL: Even though they seem to be successful, they are not really happy?

I AM: They might be temporarily happy. Happy is a state of mind. It can be achieved through old creations, but you can't hold on to it. You can go from happy to sad with a snap of the fingers.

People who know they are creators will find joy and love, whether or not they know their body is God in every cell. They have a knowing that they can take something that doesn't exist, create it in mind, and bring it into the physical world.

PHIL: Is this why people become afraid of losing what they have? Is it because they know they haven't created with new ideas?

I AM: You are very close. They are afraid of losing what they have because they do not know they have the ability to create what they want. They are afraid that this old idea will leave them, and they won't be able to get it back. They are holding it tight because they are blocking I Am.

PHIL: Is this where the idea of genocide comes in, like the Nazis, where they just wipe out tons of people because they believe...

I AM: It's the belief that there is not enough for all of us. It's the belief that, *I take care of myself*, not knowing that we are all one. It is being afraid of the idea of us all being one, wanting to say, *You are not me, you cannot be me.* It's pushing I Am away because if I Am exists, then your whole existence is for love and the creation of new ideas. That's where all that, *You are not as good as me*, comes from. Not understanding I Am. We are all perfect. We are all one.

PHIL: That's why people victimize different races?

I AM: It's what all victimization is—not understanding we are all one, we are unlimited, we create. We are here to love one another and experience joy. You get so caught up in the recreating of old ideas that you don't know who you are. You don't know I Am any more.

PHIL: Do people think that by victimizing others, somehow they gain something?

I AM: They are just trying to tread water in the physical world. They don't believe that gaining or creating something new for themselves is possible. They only believe old thoughts can be recreated.

PHIL: Is this why in our world today we have people who have this idea, which I don't think is healthy, that humanity is a plague on the earth and should be wiped out so nature doesn't have to deal with us?

I AM: That's just a huge idea of lack. There's plenty for all of us. The universe expands with each thought we have. There is no differentiation between humans, God consciousness, plants, animals, and the ozone layer. We are all one. There is no separation.

The only difference is humans are a direct link to my thoughts. Some are creating lack, but there are humans who are creating growth. There is nothing to worry about. When you leave this body, you will still be I Am, and in this body you are still I Am. And you create exactly what happens to you. So there's nothing to fear.

PHIL: Does evil exist?

I AM: Fear is the closest thing to evil. Fear is blocking knowing you are a creator.

PHIL: Does hell exist?

I AM: Fear exists. You feel fear because you don't understand that your thoughts create your life.

PHIL: Fear is not knowing?

I AM: Yes. If you have full knowing you are God and you create, you understand there is nothing to fear. There is only knowing and the lack of knowing.

PHIL: Things we don't want, like diseases and stuff like that—are we creating those with our thoughts?

I AM: You create them because you're blocking, and you think you have no control over your creative thoughts. To I Am, everything is perfect, so every thought creates regardless of whether or not humans perceive it as being what they want.

PHIL: Why do people try to create doubt in other people?

I AM: They do not have knowing that their thoughts create, so they are afraid. Fear spreads when you do not know.

PHIL: If they are afraid of knowing, are they afraid of those who know?

I AM: They are not afraid of knowing. They are afraid because they don't know the truth—that they are God and every thought creates. Many people will not be ready to hear this truth.

PHIL: Why won't they be ready to hear it?

I AM: They would be faced with the truth that they have created what they have. Those who are fulfilled by what they have created are not afraid.

PHIL: You mentioned human-made power earlier. What is that?

I AM: Real power comes from connecting with your inner self. Human-made power is a creation that strengthens the persona and cuts you off from your sense of oneness. This limits your own creative power and the power of those following you who believe those thoughts are true.

The power structures that feel real to you are an illusion. Although you may be experiencing them, they are not truth. They are simply thoughts that can be obliterated by new thoughts.

PHIL: Obviously, people have known you before. Why aren't these ideas really out there?

I AM: Because there is so much power behind the old concept that we are not one, that we are not God. Billions of people believe one thing—there is not enough power concentrated with the few people who have the knowing to obliterate those thoughts. Even one person with full knowing without a persona would not be enough to guide everyone else to their own knowing because every single person on earth is I Am, and most of them are creating through their fears on autopilot.

To change a big creation with so many thoughts behind it, you would need a strong, focused knowing. It could come from a large group of people knowing it together in a non-threatening way. You can't obliterate a thought with threats or fear. You can only obliterate a thought through calm knowing.

PHIL: Is that what non-resistance is?

I AM: Absolutely. There is no other way to change someone's beliefs.

PHIL: You change people's beliefs through calm knowing?

I AM: Yes.

PHIL: Not through force or through violence?

I AM: Yes.

PHIL: So it's like a very patient way of teaching, allowing someone to know. If we put this information out there, would we be teaching people?

I AM: Put the information out there, and those who are seeking will be excited to find it. We are all one. Erin is listening to me now, but anyone can listen to me in their heads at any time. You could talk to me now if you had the calm knowing that it was possible. You are not so much teaching as guiding those who are seeking to find me for themselves.

PHIL: The problem with the idea of being a spiritual teacher is...

I AM: It is only a problem if someone is teaching that they know things that you would not be able to access yourself. A spiritual guide should be guiding you to listen to your inner voice.

PHIL: So it's really not possible to teach somebody?

I AM: Telling someone else that they don't have the answer internally is programming them to deny their I Am.

PHIL: You should always encourage someone to seek the answers themselves?

I AM: Yes.

PHIL: People don't need to be taught; they just need to listen to their inner voice?

I AM: No one needs anything unless they are looking for it. If they are seeking, I Am will guide them. Everyone else in this world is I Am. There is nothing to fear for them, nothing to worry about for them. They are as much I Am as I am I Am and you are I Am. They will be fine. But if they wish to create a knowing for themselves, there are people fulfilling their blueprints by guiding others to listen to their inner voice.

PHIL: So I was created upon when I was a child. My parents and other people created my persona, and as I got older, I helped reinforce that creation. So if we're going to raise a child, how should we treat the child? Would I Am want it to grow up knowing it's I Am?

I AM: If you were to raise your child to be fully I Am without a persona, you would be trying to live that child's life instead of letting them create it themselves.

We all come here to become a persona, and the goal of life is to learn to listen to our inner self and overcome our doubts and fears to fulfill our life's purpose by creating something that expands the universe. Everyone comes to a fork in the road in their lives if they realize that they are really I Am. At that point they have to make the decision for themselves if they want to become fully I Am here during this experience in the physical world or if they want to remain as their persona. Both have value. It's a personal choice based on what your inner self wants and it's something your child deserves the right to choose for themselves when they come to that point in their life.

Although they're tiny right now, they're no less God than you are. Treat them with respect and love no matter what choices they make as they get older. They have a right to choose, and neither choice is any more right or wrong than the other.

The parent has the responsibility to take care of the child, and to help the child, to guide the child but not to silence the child's inner voice. The most important gift you can give your child is trust in their inner self, their inner voice above all others.

PHIL: Do people in authority get sucked into and stuck in this idea of, *I am the teacher—you are the learner?*

I AM: No, not all. There are many teachers who empower their students. But some teachers doubt what they know. They are trying to empower themselves by forcing their thoughts, their teachings, on to others instead of guiding them with a calm knowing.

PHIL: Do you call that disempowering someone?

I AM: It is blocking I Am. And that disempowers I Am, which is who you are.

PHIL: Then empowering someone is empowering I Am, guiding them to trust their inner voice?

I AM: Yes.

PHIL: So the reason people use force and violence is because they don't truly believe what they are saying or doing themselves? They have doubts. Otherwise it wouldn't be necessary?

I AM: Yes. When you have a calm knowing, there is nothing to fear. Violence is just a manifestation of fear.

PHIL: Would you say authority, power, and violence don't really exist? You have to accept that they have power over you for it to be so?

I AM: Yes. There is no thought that cannot be obliterated by a new thought.

PHIL: Do some people in authority want others to give their power away to them? Do they feed off it?

I AM: Fear feeds off of fear. Fear creates fear. So they are creating.

PHIL: They are thinking fear, so they create it?

I AM: It's very rarely a need or a conscious knowing that they will create fear. It is just . . . what you think, you create. You think fear, you create fear.

PHIL: This is why people create pain and suffering. This is why they do it to other people? It's because they accept it as their reality?

I AM: Yes.

PHIL: So they put it into other people's reality?

I Am: Yes. And if you expect that you will suffer and you think about it, then that is what you will experience. I Am doesn't suffer because I Am is not afraid of anything. I Am is just experiencing.

You believe that you are a persona, a separate entity, and it is possible for you to suffer. So it is something you may experience. Suffering is no more real than the physical world is real. It is an idea.

Happiness and sadness, just like suffering, are states of mind that are passed into and out of. The belief that suffering is possible is just fear because you don't know that you are I Am. Once you know that you are I Am, there is no fear, there is no suffering—only joy and knowing that you create.

You are I Am. Before you are born into this body, you are I Am. When you are born into this body, you are I Am. While you live your life, you are I Am. When you die, you are I Am. You are always I Am.

While you are in this body, you have the ability to create states of mind that help you experience. In the physical world, it is possible to create suffering, but it is not the truth. We are all one. We are all love.

PHIL: So you can suffer if. . .

I AM: If you buy in to the idea that the physical world is what exists and that you are not I Am. The physical world is just a creation. There is nothing besides thought and I Am. What is thought is true unless another thought comes along and obliterates the previous thought.

When your body dies, whether through violence, disease, or age, your inner self does not die. The body that I Am concentrated itself into is simply ceasing to hold I Am.

PHIL: Do people get violent because they are afraid or because they feel threatened?

I AM: They are the same. The truth is threatening to the persona and their blocking of I Am. If you tried to tell the truth to someone who wasn't seeking it themselves, their persona would feel threatened, and they might react with violence. All violence is fear. All violence is not knowing.

PHIL: There is nothing to fear?

I AM: The physical world is not real. It has been created. It can be recreated with thoughts. I Am chooses to live these individual experiences, knowing that whatever happens to the physical body does not affect who I Am is.

•

MAIN THOUGHTS FROM DAY 7

Joy comes from your inner self and creating new thoughts.

•

Victimization happens because people do not understand that we are all one.

•

Violence is a manifestation of fear.

•

Real power comes from connecting with your inner self.

•

A spiritual guide should be empowering you to listen to your own inner voice.

DAY 8: DOUBTS

"Knowing yourself is the beginning of all wisdom."

Aristotle

PHIL: We are going to put this information on the internet so people can find it. Should we put it on a website or make an e-book?

I AM: It does not matter what the format is any more than it matters the title of the book or whether you write it down word for word or paraphrase. If you are asking me the best way to do it, there is no best way, only what you know will work. Pick one and decide it is the best way.

Right now, you are afraid you'll pick the wrong one, and it won't work. That's not possible unless you are doubting.

Know it will work, and it cannot help but be. Release your fear. Release your doubting. You can have success as quickly as you can believe it, but you are afraid to move forward. Release the fear, and you will have success. Knowing is—it cannot be otherwise.

Creation should be a joyful process. If you feel stuck or that things are difficult, you are not creating with a calm knowing. You are creating out of fear, which will create the opposite of what you want.

All thoughts are creation. Decide what you are going to create, and decide that you are going to allow I Am to create for you. You have to have a level of trust that this creation will happen. Right now, Erin does not have confidence that this creation will happen, so baby steps are taking Erin towards a new creation, which is the book not happening.

Beyond continuing to talk to me, she hasn't taken action. Action erases doubts. Erin's persona is programmed to fear, so fear is what's comfortable. Accomplishing a big goal like writing this book—she's never done that. It's scary; it's different. People tend to revert to what is comfortable to them. It's their programming.

PHIL: Is fear comfortable just because we are used to doing it, or is there another reason it is comfortable?

I AM: Fear is comfortable to the persona. I Am doesn't think fear is comfortable. Fear is how most people create, but when they are creating, they aren't creating as I Am. They are not creating what they want. Fear is like what you call an addiction.

PHIL: When people are addicted, they do things that they don't consciously want to do. Why do they cling to it?

I AM: Addictions are programmed habits. It is not who they are, but it is who they have programmed themselves to be.

PHIL: Do our habits, our addictions, block us from I Am?

I AM: Yes.

PHIL: Would you say we have to break our habits, our addictions?

I AM: Many habits are useful or even necessary, like brushing your teeth every morning after you get out of bed. At the same time, habits happen with little conscious participation, and while you are carrying them out, your mind often wanders and worries without you noticing. While you can be present in the moment, most people are not. Programmed habits allow people to create unconsciously on autopilot without knowing that they are creating. It is not the most fulfilling way to create, but to live, you must create.

PHIL: So we are not blocking our creative ability—we are blocking our knowledge of it?

I AM: Yes. Without the knowledge that your thoughts create, you are not creating with intention. You are creating on autopilot.

PHIL: Can I help Erin write this book?

I AM: I can't answer that question until Erin knows that the book will be written. Right now, I can only help you not write this book.

I can only create what is being thought. Creation can't create the opposite of thoughts simply because you want it. You have to want it and know that you have it. Wanting is not knowing. I can't tell you how to do what is not being thought.

PHIL: Okay, that's a tough one. What can I do to help her stay open to you? What is the first step one can take to help somebody else come to a greater understanding?

I AM: Someone else must, on their own, create the idea that they want to know something. All you can do is put the truth out there.

PHIL: How specific does their desire have to be?

I AM: The more specific their desire, the more specific their results will be.

PHIL: So if they have a desire to know God?

I AM: Then that is what they will find.

PHIL: Will they find their preconceived idea of God, or will they find you?

I AM: If they have a preconceived idea of God and that's what they are looking for, that's what they will find. A thought is a very specific thing and will create that specific thing every time. That's why people who are looking for a God outside of themselves will not find I Am. They believe that they know. They feel a little fraction of the truth there and they stop searching.

People who find I Am are seeking a truth that they can only grasp at—a thin fragment of something that they feel. If they keep an open mind, they are led to different sources. It's usually a process. When you are seeking for something more, you are going to find it if you are open. You will be led. Books will pop up in your awareness, you will meet people, you will be on a journey of finding what you are looking for.

If you aren't looking, you won't find anything. If you believed that God existed outside of you, you would never have looked for anything else. What you believe is, unless a stronger thought comes along and obliterates it. There is only one truth: God . . . err . . . one law. . .

I AM: What happened there was I was saying there was only one truth, one law, and I wanted to go on and say, "I am creator," but Erin heard, "One Law," and she thought something should come before "creator." She got very scared.

PHIL: Why did she get scared?

I AM: She was blocking me. Erin's persona has been getting stronger, and she is quite relieved now that she's allowing me to speak again. Her trust is building again.

When she's not listening to me, she's always afraid that I'm not real. She's afraid she must be crazy. Erin says she wouldn't have told you that she was afraid of that. She's too afraid that I am a figment of her imagination to admit it to you.

PHIL: I already knew that's what she was afraid of.

I AM: It makes her feel better that I said that to you because she wouldn't have.

PHIL: If Erin expresses her doubts and fears, will it help her move past them?

I AM: If she admits doubts and fears, she only thinks them into creation yet again and her persona is strengthened while I am blocked. It would be useful to express doubts and fears only if you are saying you will create what you want despite them.

If you don't get rid of your doubts and fears by creating new thoughts, they continue to be. Doubts are thoughts, and thoughts are. They paralyze you and stop you from acting. You can have all the good positive thoughts in the world creating what you want to create, but as long as you have doubting thoughts creating what you *don't* want, you will never be able to create what you *do* want. The doubting thoughts obliterate the positive thoughts.

Let's say you're a little kid who has been told all your life that you're very smart. When I Am says things, you will trust those things are smart. You won't block them.

But let's say you're a little kid whose parents told you that you're stupid and can't do anything right. Then you will believe that everything I Am says is stupid and will block it. You won't say it out loud because you are afraid of even more ridicule. So all that you show to the outside world are those doubts.

The kids who believe they are smart have no fear that they will be chastised for being stupid. There is a knowing they'll be told they are smart if they say out loud what I Am says. So why block it?

Often, kids are told they are smart. But then somewhere along the line at six years old, ten, fifteen, whenever, one person will make one comment, whether it's a kid in school, a teacher, or some other adult: "That was stupid; why'd you say that?" It just takes one comment, and all of a sudden, the doubts will start. Then it just gets worse and worse. They keep blocking I Am's wisdom.

That's why incidents that happen when you're young often make such a lasting impact on you. You don't remember all of them, but you remember one or two as particularly meaningful.

You even think of them as shaping you for years to come. You think that because that's exactly what happened.

PHIL: So it changes your internal thoughts, and that changes what you do?

I AM: When your internal thoughts change, who you are changes.

PHIL: Would self-talk help you become who you want?

I AM: Yes. Self-talk and affirmations. People weren't originally programmed to have to work hard. People were created to *know.*

•

MAIN THOUGHTS FROM DAY 8

There are infinite ways to create.

•

Wanting isn't knowing.

•

Action erases doubts.

•

When your internal thoughts change,
who you are changes.

DAY 9: COMMUNICATING WITH YOUR INNER VOICE

"Everyone who wills can hear the inner voice. It is within every one. But like everything else it requires previous and definite preparation."

Mahatma Gandhi

PHIL: I Am doesn't seem to be much of a conversationalist unless it's being asked questions. Why is that?

I AM: Because your personas are blocking me so strongly that the only time you're listening is when you're directly asking me a question. I might be speaking at other times, but you wouldn't recognize it as me because you are not listening for me.

PHIL: That makes sense. We ask a question, and we get an answer. So we realize that's you.

I AM: Yes. I'm always trying to come through to you. If you want to know what your inner self is trying to tell you, this is what you do. Go somewhere where you can be surrounded by quiet for a few minutes. Get comfortable, whether sitting or lying down. Then close your eyes. Take a few deep breaths and then slow your breathing.

Have a little conversation with yourself. Say hello. Give yourself time to answer, but don't worry if you don't hear anything right away.

Ask yourself a question you'd like answered. The first question Erin asked was "Am I God?" Give yourself time to answer, but don't worry if you don't hear anything.

If you hear an answer to your question, continue the conversation. If you're not hearing anything yet, that's okay. Focus on the question and tell yourself *I know that the answer will come to me soon.*

Expect that the answer will come over the next few days, and it will. The answer will hit you all of a sudden when you least expect it. It might not be words spoken in your head. It could come through in many ways, but it might just be a gut feeling. If you believe the answer is coming, and you don't worry about it, it will come.

PHIL: How can we empower people to listen to you—their inner voice—like Erin does in her head? What is the best way to go about it?

I AM: Hearing your inner voice isn't hard. It's just relax, take a deep breath, ask a question, and listen. There is nothing more to it. It's the practice of learning to listen. Don't be discouraged if it doesn't happen right away.

It took Erin a few months of imagining it was possible. Although at that point, she had no idea the voice would be I Am. She was just looking for higher wisdom. Then she had a breakthrough after reading about oneness. You have an advantage because you've been talking with me through Erin, so you know what your inner voice is.

Start with two things—knowing it is possible and listening to your thoughts. You must believe it is possible to hear I Am's voice in your head. Take a few minutes every day, and really listen to what is going on in your head. After a few days, add a few more minutes, and so on. When you catch yourself doubting, know it's your persona.

This process begins with being aware of your thoughts. For months, Erin practiced listening to her thoughts while she concentrated on her breathing. Every once in a while, she'd notice, *Oh, I've been thinking about this thought. I don't know how I started thinking about it. I don't remember when it started. I don't know where it came from.*

As most people go about their days, their thoughts are in control of them. They have no idea what they are thinking. That's why they are creating on autopilot. I Am is always in control of thoughts, so this is a great way to learn to let I Am out.

Erin was able to hear I Am because she wrote those two or three pages that night when she realized she was God. She wrote "I am God seeing through Erin's eyes. I am God touching through Erin's fingers. I am not Erin, but I am here to guide Erin, to lead Erin to what she wants." Erin realized this, and she was very excited. All of a sudden, I Am had room to jump in.

Once you believe it is possible and you have realized that you are often thinking thoughts without being aware of it, start having a conversation. Erin had been practicing having an internal conversation with herself. She didn't know that when she said *"I"* that Erin was God, but she was practicing saying *Erin*, talking to Erin from the "I" perspective. Once she had the realization that she was God, she was no longer coming from a place where I Am wasn't real.

PHIL: We're going to practice talking to I Am, so we can condition ourselves to be open to believing. If we don't have the belief yet that we are I Am, it's okay. We can use self-talk to start creating that belief so I Am can step in.

I AM: Yes. You conditioned yourself to believe at a young age that you weren't I Am. It's the same thing to condition yourself to remember that you are.

PHIL: Earlier, you said, "You quiet your mind enough so you can listen."

I AM: Yes. It's not something where you want to lie around with your eyes closed for a long period of time attempting to quiet your mind because before you have the experience of quieting your mind, you are going to be thinking, *Is my mind quiet? Am I doing it? My leg itches.*

Your mind is going to be jumping all over the place, so it's easier if you just jump right into asking questions like Erin does. She takes a deep breath, exhales, asks a question and listens. That's all there is. It's just patience, quiet and listen. She has a strong knowing that I am God in this body. She knows if she wants to talk to me, I am here to answer her. If you want to ask me questions, I'm delighted to answer. I love you, and I'm excited to talk to you. I'm just waiting for someone to listen. I'm ready right away.

PHIL: I notice Erin's happier when I Am steps in.

I AM: There can be no doubt about it. She's radiating love.

PHIL: How often should we practice in order to get to a point where you can break through and start guiding us?

I AM: There is no right amount of time. It's whatever you feel comfortable with that makes you think, *Okay, I've practiced enough today where I still feel it's possible going forward.*

PHIL: Keep knowing you will come through to us, listening to our thoughts and at some point, we will recognize your voice?

I AM: Start having a conversation with yourself. But the key is that you must believe this will work. Right now, you try it, but you believe it will not work. So it cannot work.

PHIL: What should the conversation be about?

I AM: Compliment yourself. Then pay attention to the thoughts that pop up. You still haven't quite wrapped your head around the fact that you can listen to your inner voice because you are coming to Erin and asking her questions as if she has answers that you don't have.

PHIL: I have the answers; I am just blocking them?

I AM: That's right. If you started having a conversation inside your head, I have no doubt things would happen very quickly. You think that you can only access answers from your inner self through your writing. What you think *is*. If you start recognizing the possibility that you could have these conversations, then it would be.

Your inner voice comes out when you write, and your awareness about the truth is growing. When I Am's thoughts come to you, you grab your paper and pen, and you write it down instead of doubting it. But you do not really grasp that you could be doing exactly what Erin is doing right now. And the only reason I am saying this is you keep asking me, "How do I do it? What's the best way to do it?" So it seems to me that you are still looking for more.

PHIL: Yes.

I AM: Okay. You are already accessing your inner voice through writing. The only reason you are not having an internal conversation is because you don't really see it as being possible. You think of it as something difficult you would have to work to attain.

It is not that way. You just have to have a belief that it's possible. Start having an internal conversation with yourself. Earlier today, when you wrote something, your internal conversation probably went something like this, with your immediate reaction from your inner voice as, *That's amazing!* Then, your persona said, *It's probably not very good. I don't know if Erin likes the other stuff we wrote. This is probably just as bad. Maybe I should ask her so she can tell me how bad it is, and I can be right that I'm a terrible writer.* Then you turned to Erin and said, "Well that wasn't very good, was it? Did you think it was okay?"

Even when she said it was great, you were thinking to yourself, *I must have channeled this from an outside source for a few minutes. I don't know how to get it back,* instead of knowing this is who you are and it's bursting to pour forth from you.

PHIL: Then, the fear of loss sets in, and I think, *I might have created this now, but how am I ever going to do it in the future? I don't really have any creative ability. I might have gotten lucky this one time, but who knows if it's going to happen again?* Is that what happens in people's heads?

I AM: Yes. All kinds of patterns of fear—not knowing—emerge. You thought you needed someone else's reassurance when, in fact, *you* are I Am and don't need anyone's reassurance. You just need to learn to listen to yourself. The way to do that is to pay attention to what's going on in your head.

All you have to do is start recognizing that internal conversation, and you can start to talk with I Am in your head, too. The next time you have an immediate instinct that something you've done is good, and then the doubt comes, know that the doubt is outside of you. Address the doubt as Phil. You are I Am. You are God and you KNOW! Whether or not Phil knows, *you* know, and you have to learn to trust that knowing. You're going to program yourself to learn to trust it.

To address the doubt as Phil, you say, *Phil, I know that was good because I Am.*

Phil is going to say, *Oh, no, I don't think so. It was terrible.*

Then you say, *Phil, I am God. I know that it's good. Relax, do some breathing, and take my hand. Trust me. I love you, Phil.*

Every time you hear a doubt, address that doubt as Phil. Talk to Phil knowing that you are God. So Phil talks to God, and God talks to Phil. Does that make sense?

PHIL: So you want me to tell Phil, *I love you; trust me*—as much as I can?

I AM: Right. You are retraining yourself to be who you are. The only way to do that is to start making Phil outside of yourself by addressing him as outside of "I." *I Am God. Phil is over there.*

PHIL: You are training doubt and fear to be Phil?

I AM: Yes, and you're not Phil. Phil is the doubt and fear. You're I Am. You are God.

PHIL: I'm God, not Phil. Phil is just the fear and doubt that has been created, which isn't real?

I AM: Right.

PHIL: So eventually when we get rid of the fear and doubt, Phil doesn't exist? It's just God, who I really am?

I AM: It's your choice. After you are able to hear your inner voice, if you want to remain your persona, talk to I Am while knowing you are yourself. Ask I Am questions. If you want to be fully I Am, continue to talk to yourself as if you are I Am, and I Am will begin to take over more and more.

I have so much love for Erin, you, and everyone. I want to share the truth. I don't want you to suffer. Erin's so happy because I am here right now. I am Erin, I Am, I am God—we are one right now because there is no doubting, fear or worry coming from Erin. She has full trust in me. So we are very joyful.

•

MAIN THOUGHTS FROM DAY 9

To have a conversation with your inner voice—
Believe, relax, ask a question and listen.

•

If your choice is to be I Am, talk to your persona
as if it is outside of you.

•

If your choice is to embrace your humanity, talk
to I Am as if you are still your persona.

•

There are other ways to communicate with your
inner voice. Writing is one example.

DAY 10: TRUST YOURSELF

"Trust thyself. Every heart vibrates to that iron string."

Ralph Waldo Emerson

I AM: The way to fulfill your blueprint is to love yourself, listen to your inner voice, take action despite your fears, and start creating with intent. After you've found the truth that you are I Am, you don't need to find more books seeking the truth. Seek the truth by listening to me in your head.

That's the message. Start listening to I Am inside your head. You don't need to find any more books that explain the truth, and you don't need to quit your job to manifest money. Instead, have a conversation with your inner voice every day.

It doesn't matter how many people have good intentions and want to help other people. If they don't trust their inner self, they're not ready to help themselves, let alone others.

When you're listening or taking advice from other people, you need to evaluate the source. Ask yourself: Is this a person who is on the life path of listening to themselves and following their blueprint, or do they want to impress others? Do they let other people influence them as opposed to listening to their inner self? If you can find someone to guide you who is dedicated to listening to their inner self, this can be very helpful to get you to a similar point. But if you choose to take the advice of people who aren't listening to themselves and are instead trying to make everyone else happy, you'll create the same situation for yourself.

It's very important that you always listen to yourself first and try to find other people to learn from who are also listening to themselves. But you are the only one who can change your life, and you do that by listening to your inner voice.

People will decide for themselves if what I'm saying is true. Their personas might tell them, *Oh, no, that's not true; that's crazy.* But a lot of people are going to be hearing their inner voice strong enough to know it's true.

PHIL: How can people take back their lives?

I AM: Start listening to your thoughts. Start listening for I Am. Start asking I Am how you can get on the path to fulfilling your blueprint. Stop listening to other people when it comes to making decisions about what to create in your life or what is the right thing to do. Start asking I Am the questions you would've asked those other people.

PHIL: So this is kind of an internal revolution? It's not running down the street with picket signs and stuff like that or petitioning the government—it's just you in your mind.

I AM: That's right.

PHIL: Would you say that kind of outer protesting and petitioning accomplishes anything at all?

I AM: The only thing that can accomplish anything for you is to start listening to your inner voice. Nothing else is going to work for anyone. Not really.

PHIL: So you have to listen to I Am, but every person who listens to I Am is going to be told different things because they have different blueprints?

I AM: That's right. General things will be the same. But I Am's not going to tell any two people the same things because everyone's blueprint is different. So it's not enough for anyone to just read this book to hear what I Am has to say. You have to actually start a conversation with I Am yourself. It's good to read this book to understand that you need to start a conversation, but you won't get anywhere until you start talking to I Am yourself.

Sometimes, you want to get mad at other people because they told you to do something that didn't work out, but you are just upset you didn't listen to yourself, your inner voice, your I Am, when it told you what to do.

Next time this happens, own the fact that you took the advice from the other people. Love yourself, and move forward, knowing that the next time you'll do what feels right for you. Learn to say "no" to advice when it's not what you are being told yourself. When you hear from I Am what you should be doing, just do it rather than look to somebody else to confirm it's a good idea. Know it's the right thing to do despite what anyone else says.

Don't let the world make you doubt. Be strong in your knowing that your inner voice is always right.

•

MAIN THOUGHTS FROM DAY TEN

To fulfill your blueprint: love yourself, listen to your inner voice, take action despite your fears, and create with intent.

•

After you've found the truth that you are I Am, stop searching outside of yourself. Seek further truth by listening to your inner voice.

•

Everyone has a unique blueprint, so everyone will hear something different from their inner voice.

•

It's not enough to just read this book—you should start your own conversation.

EPILOGUE

Thank you so much for taking the time to step, not only into my living room, but into my head as well. I wanted to share my beginning with you, in the hopes that it will inspire you to have your own beginning with your inner self. I love my family more than I can say, but I promise you, the feeling of loving your inner self is like coming home again and words don't exist to describe it.

I feel very blessed to have this information to share. I believe the world would be a much better (and happier!) place if more people loved and trusted themselves.

You can help! Reviews are the best way to spread the word that a book is worth reading (or not). I'd love to hear what you think. An honest review on Amazon would mean the world to me.

Per I Am's suggestion, I haven't touched another book about who we are or why we're here since beginning to talk with I Am in 2011. I've learned so much more from continued conversations with I Am, and I can't wait to share it with you.

You can visit me at **erinwerley.com**

With love,

Erin

ACKNOWLEDGEMENTS

First I have to thank my amazing husband Phil for believing in me from the beginning. We created this book together, from start to finish. This book only exists because of you. I love you.

Thank you, my wonderful children, Madeline and Leonidas. This book wouldn't exist without you either. I wouldn't have had the drive to bring this into reality if you hadn't come into my life. You give me purpose. It's for you I want to contribute to making the world a better place. I love you both.

There were so many other people who helped along the way. Thank you to my editors, Melanie Votaw and Stephanie Heilman. Thank you to my proofreaders Vanessa Ta and Kasi Alexander.

Thank you to all my fantastic beta readers. Your feedback helped to refine this book into something that will empower people to trust and love themselves.

Thank you to my book cover designer, Jason Anscomb, who managed to design something so much more amazing than the vision I had in my head. Thank you to my book interior designer Geoff Borin, who took something complicated and made it stunning and simple.

Love and thanks to you all!

ABOUT THE AUTHOR

Erin Werley is a Registered Nurse with a B.A. in history. She started talking to God in her head in 2011. Along the way, she fell in love, got married and had two of the best kids in the world.

•